bracelets

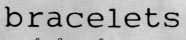

bracelets

by Joan Gordon

Guild of Master
Craftsman Publications

First published 2011 by
Guild of Master Craftsman Publications Ltd
Castle Place, 166 High Street, Lewes,
East Sussex BN7 1XU

Text © Joan Gordon, 2011
Copyright in the Work © GMC Publications Ltd, 2011

Reprinted 2012

ISBN 978 1 86108 876 5

Publisher Jonathan Bailey
Production Manager Jim Bulley
Managing Editor Gerrie Purcell
Editor Beth Wicks
Managing Art Editor Gilda Pacitti
Art Editor Rebecca Mothersole
Designer Sarah Howerd
Photographer Rebecca Mothersole

Set in King and Myriad
Colour origination by GMC
Reprographics
Printed and bound in China by
Hing Yip

PLIERS

EYEPINS AND HEADPINS

WRAPPED LOOPS

contents

Tools and Materials

Techniques

CLASPS

CRIMPING

SILVER CLASPS

JUMPRINGS AND SPLIT RINGS

DRILLING AND HAMMERING

FLORENCE

ZOË

SUNNY

PEPPER

YAHN

ROSE

PEARL

The Projects

PEBBLES

MINNI

SHELLY

MILLE

ANNIE

JOULES

MISS JANE

AMY

JAN

CHELSEA

GEMMA

DAISY

SKY

Tools and Materials

This visual resource will be of assistance when you are gathering materials and tools together to assemble the bracelet of your choice. The following chapter on techniques will show you how the basic tools and equipment are used in jewellery making.

pliers

ROUND-NOSE

These pliers have rounded jaws that taper towards the end. They are used for making eyepins, wrapped loops and for shaping wire.

FLAT-NOSE

These pliers have a flat nose, while the jaw is flat. They are handy for crimping flat ribbon crimps, opening and closing jumprings and for holding wire or jewellery components.

CHAIN-NOSE (OR SNIPE-NOSE)

These have pointed ends and are used for opening or closing links in a chain, jumprings and for wire work.

WIRE SNIPS (SNIPPERS)

Snippers are used for cutting wire and for trimming ribbons or leather.

SPLIT RING

This special tool is used for opening split rings. The jaw with the pointed tooth at the end slides between the wire rings and creates a space without distorting the spring.

CRIMPING

Crimping pliers come in various sizes. It is important to use the correct size jaw for the crimps you are using. The back of the jaw squashes the crimp, the middle section shapes it and the front rounds the flattened crimp.

TEFLON

These pliers are used in wire work to prevent marking or damaging the surface of the metal.

TOP CUTTERS

These are used for cutting wire neatly and cleanly, especially when cutting loops of wire to create jumprings. They can cut at a 90-degree angle and are therefore ideal for getting into difficult spaces.

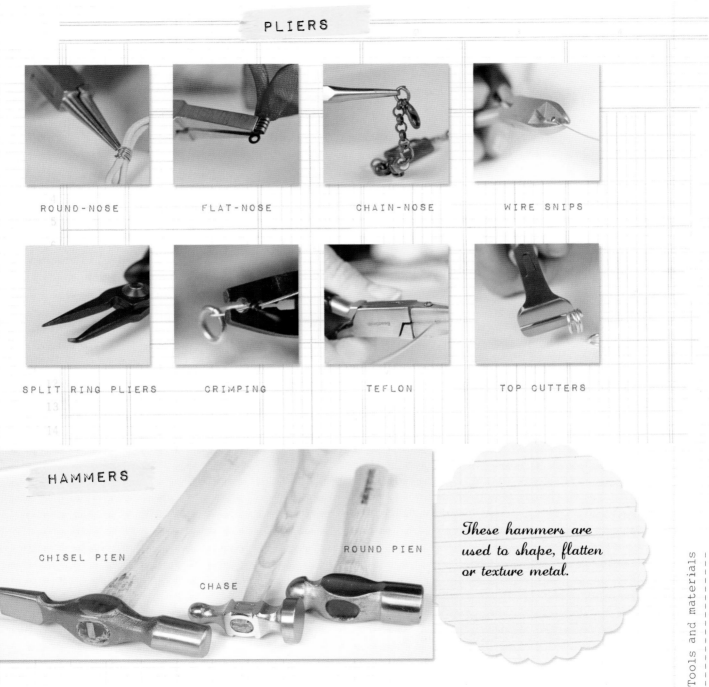

PLIERS

ROUND-NOSE

FLAT-NOSE

CHAIN-NOSE

WIRE SNIPS

SPLIT RING PLIERS

CRIMPING

TEFLON

TOP CUTTERS

HAMMERS

CHISEL PIEN

CHASE

ROUND PIEN

These hammers are used to shape, flatten or texture metal.

Tools and materials

STEEL BLOCK

A steel block is used in conjunction with a hammer to support the metal when shaping or texturing techniques are employed.

HAND DRILL

This is a handy tool for drilling holes in metal, shell, wood and other surfaces.

CANDY TORCH

This simple kitchen torch is fuelled with butane gas. It is often used in jewellery making to create headpins from fine or sterling silver. Good quality torches may also be used for soldering.

glue

EPOXY GLUE A two-part glue that when mixed together sets hard. Only use glue that is specifically designed for gluing the materials you are using. Where possible use ones that dry clear giving a professional finish.

CYANOACRYLATE A very handy resource for sealing knots, although not advisable for use on stretch illusion cord as it will cause the elastic to perish.

NAIL VARNISH Ideal for sealing the ends of ribbons, knitted wire and illusion cord.

stringing materials

There is an almost unlimited range of stringing materials on the market. It's important to use high-quality materials when stringing and linking beads together to ensure that your bracelet will last.

STRETCH ILLUSION CORD

This elastic cord is referred to as illusion due to its transparency. It is an excellent stranding material for making stretch bracelets. Use more than one strand for extra strength. These cords are available in a variety of different colours and prices – the more expensive the better the quality.

NYLON-COATED METAL STRAND

Several strands of fine micro wire threads are coated in a flexible metal finish. This product is very strong and available in several different finishes, including sterling silver and gold plate.

SUEDE AND LEATHER

If you are creating natural or ethnic-styled jewellery, consider using thin strands of suede or leather when stringing together wooden, handmade or ceramic beads. These will give the piece a tactile, earthy quality.

Stretch illusion cord is a magical thing, almost invisible, yet stretchy and strong.

SYNTHETIC CORD

This cord is made from synthetic leather. Unlike real leather it won't stretch and can be cleaned with a damp cloth. It is an inexpensive alternative to using the real thing.

RIBBON

Polyester, silk, organza, cotton and mixed-fibre ribbons make for unusual stinging materials. They can also be used as wrist bands or to replace chain or cord when finishing a bracelet. They are visually appealing and easy to replace when soiled or worn.

FINE CHAIN

Car boot sales and charity shops are ideal places in which to rummage for treasures and inexpensive chains. When using chain as a stringing material ensure that the hole in the beads is large enough for the chain to slide through.

HERE A FINE CHAIN HAS BEEN USED WITH STRETCH ILLUSION CORD TO MAKE A VERY JANGLY BRACELET

clasps

There are many different types and styles of clasps available. Those shown below are just a few of the many manufactured clasps that can be purchased from online shops or local bead stores. Alternatively, you can recycle clasps from old pieces of jewellery.

TOGGLE

This simple clasp is ideal for securing chain-link bracelets. The toggle bar slides into the circular clasp where it lies against the edges of the circle to keep the bracelet fastened.

MAGNETIC

These clasps make fastening a bracelet very easy, especially one that is decorated with lots of charms. The clasps are attached to each end of the bracelet, and the two magnetic poles are attracted to each other snapping the bracelet shut.

PARROT (LOBSTER)

This spring-loaded clasp looks like a parrot's beak or the claws of a lobster hence its name. It is made in a variety of different sizes and metals and is worked with a little side lever. The clasp is fastened to one end of a bracelet and connects to a jumpring attached to the other end to close the piece.

FANCY

Using a fancy clasp to a bracelet adds charm and originality to the piece. Look for a variety of clasps and store them in your jewellery stash. That way you'll always have something on hand to add designer detail to your work.

MAGNETIC

PARROT

FANCY

#

crimping

A crimp is a soft metal bead or flat open finding that is folded or pressed closed over stringing material to secure the ends. If you don't have crimping pliers to hand, use flat-nose pliers to secure the stringing material and the crimp. The crimp should be large enough to thread over the stringing material, yet small enough to secure the threads when pressed closed.

BASIC CRIMPS

The basic round or tubular crimp bead comes in a variety of different sizes and coloured metals.

1 To link a strand of threading material onto a jumpring, or to make a loop in the end of threading material, slide a crimp onto the end of the wire/thread you are using.

2 Pass the stringing material through the jumpring, then double it back onto itself. Thread the end of the wire back through the crimp bead creating a small loop.

3 Slide the crimp upwards towards the end of the loop. Place it in the crimping pliers jaw and use the back of the jaw to press the crimp flat. Next, move it to the middle of the wire to kink it.

4 To finish, turn the crimp vertical and place it into the front of the jaws. This will round off the crimp.

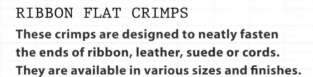

CALOTTES (FRENCH CRIMPS)

Calottes look like an open clam shell with a tail. The stringing material is passed through a hole in the base, then crimped. The calotte is closed to cover the crimped bead. These fancy crimps are used for covering round crimps and to make the ends of strung beads look neat.

1. Thread the end of the stringing material through the central hole on the base of the calotte.

2. Slide a crimp bead onto the end of the material. Make a tiny loop and pass the end through the crimp and back out of the hole in the base of the calotte. Press the bead closed with crimping, flat or chain-nose pliers.

3. Using the pliers, gently close the calotte closed over the crimped end.

4. The end of the calotte can now be attached to a linked bead, jumpring or clasp.

RIBBON FLAT CRIMPS

These crimps are designed to neatly fasten the ends of ribbon, leather, suede or cords. They are available in various sizes and finishes.

1. Place the end of the ribbon or cord into the centre of the crimp. Paint the end of the stringing material with clear nail varnish to prevent it from fraying.

2. Using flat-nose or chain-nose pliers, press one edge of the crimp closed over the stringing material.

3. Close the other side of the crimp and press firmly with the pliers to secure it into place.

4. Attach a jumpring and clasp to the end of the flat crimp.

jumprings and split rings

Jumprings and split rings are both used to connect beads and findings.

JUMPRINGS

A jumpring is a single ring of metal that springs closed to secure the item into place. In cold linking it is not soldered into place, instead it is simply closed with a pair of pliers.

1 To open a jumpring, grip it firmly in a pair of pliers with the opening at the top of the ring. Then twist the pliers towards or away from you. If you open the ring outwards the metal ring will distort and loose its spring and may possibly cause it to break.

2 To close the jumpring, twist the pliers in the opposite direction to when you open it. Press the pliers in towards each other so that the join of the ring clicks closed. The join should be as close and neat as possible.

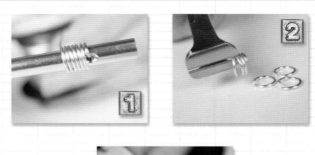

MAKING JUMPRINGS

1 To make several jumprings, wind a length of wire around a round object, keeping the spirals close together. For strong rings use $1/32$in (0.8mm) wire.

2 Slide the coil of rings off and clip them apart down the centre of the spring using sharp wire snips or top cutters. Always use very sharp tools, as the cleaner the cut, the better the closure of the ring.

3 When only one or two jumprings are required, wrap a length of wire a few times around the jaws of round-nose pliers. Slide the spring of wire from off the jaws and clip the coil into single rings.

SPLIT RINGS

A split ring is a small coil of wire used when a more secure connection is required.

1   To open a split ring, slide the point of the split ring pliers between the coils of the ring.

2   Slide the end of the ring onto the jumpring, eyepin, clasp or wrapped loop that you wish to link it up with.

3   Turn the ring until it is securely linked with the item. The spring will close when you reach the central loop in the ring.

MAKING SPLIT RINGS

1   Split rings are made in the same way as jumprings, the only difference is when you come to cut them. First, wrap three coils of wire around a round object.

2   Cut the first and third coil of wire so that the ring has a half coil of wire at the start and end with a full ring of wire in the centre.

eyepins

Eyepins and headpins are used to create decorative drops or to link jewellery pieces together. They are available in various metals, lengths and thicknesses. When using an eyepin or a headpin, an eye needs to be made at the other end of the pin to hold the beads in place.

EYEPINS

An eyepin is a straight piece of wire with a P-shaped coil, called an eye, at one end. If you haven't got an eyepin to hand, simply cut a piece of wire to the desired length and make an eye at one end of it. Thread the beads onto it and make a similar eye at the other end.

MAKING EYEPINS

1   Thread the beads or jewellery items onto the eyepin. Using pliers make a right-angled bend in the wire that extends from the end bead. Make the bend as close to the bead as possible.

2   For a large eye, use wire snips to cut off all but $3/8$in (10mm) of wire. To make a smaller eye, cut it to a length of approximately $1/4$–$9/32$in (6–7mm).

3   Hold the wire in the jaws of some round-nose pliers. Choose an area on the jaw that will give you the size of the eye you require. Then, roll your wrist, twisting the wire into a half coil. Release the wire and move the pliers around the coil before regripping it. Continue to roll the coil to form a P-shaped eye. Use flat-nose pliers to centre the eye above the bead.

CONNECTORS

It is easy to create simple connecters to link jumprings and beaded eyepins together. Use wire straight from a spool or off-cuts from other jewellery making projects. As the old saying goes, waste not, want not.

MAKING CONNECTORS

1   Using round-nose pliers grab the very end of the wire. Twist your wrist to make the start of an S-shape. This small coil should be sufficiently large to connect securely with a jumpring. Concentrate on where you have gripped it, as the second coil should be made in the same position.

2   Measure down $9/_{32}$in (7mm) from the end of the coil, then cut off the extending wire with metal snippers.

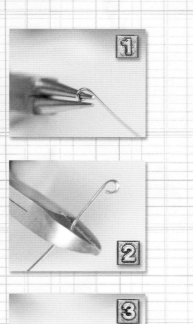

headpins

Headpins can be made from sterling silver or fine silver wire. With sterling silver, the pin will have to be pickled once it is made in order to remove the oxidization. Fine silver doesn't tarnish, so it is the easiest one to use.

SAFETY TIPS

- READ THE INSTRUCTIONS FOR THE TORCH BEFORE IGNITION

- ALWAYS PIN BACK LONG HAIR

- USE PLIERS WITH INSULATED HANDLES TO PREVENT BURNING YOUR FINGERS ON THE HOT WIRE

- KEEP A GLASS OF WATER HANDY TO COOL THE HEADPINS ONCE MADE

- A CAN OF BURN SPRAY IS A GOOD IDEA TO HAVE ON HAND

- WORK ON A FIREPROOF SURFACE, SUCH AS A SLATE TILE

MAKING HEADPINS

1 Use a tape measure to determine the length of the headpin you wish to make.

2 Cut the wire at the required length using wire snips.

3 Light a candy torch and hold one end of the wire with fire-proof pliers. Place the other end vertically in the flame. Hold the wire in the flame until the end glows red and the wire melts into a ball.

4 When you have created a ball large enough to stop the bead from falling off turn off the flame. Do not touch the wire! Drop the wire headpin into cold water. It is now ready for use.

wrapped loops

A wrapped loop is used as a secure method for attaching beads or charms to a headpin or eyepin. They are made in a similar way to eyepins, although the wire is wrapped around the pin a few times to ensure that the beads cannot fall off. To make a wrapped loop, use wire that is soft and easy to manipulate. The harder the wire, the more difficult it is to manipulate.

MAKING WRAPPED LOOPS

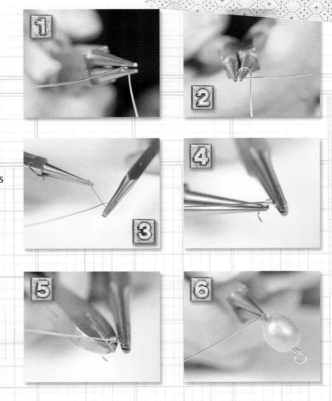

1   Cut a length of wire approximately three times the length of the bead. Use round-nose or flat-nose pliers to make a right-angle bend at one end. Leave approximately ³/₄in (20mm) of wire to create the wrap with.

2   Hold the wire in the jaws of some round-nose pliers, approximately ³/₄in (20mm) down from one end. Roll the wire into a semi-circle, then release it from the jaws and regrip it. Roll the wire into a P-shape. Ensure that the end of the wire crosses the main body of the wire at a right angle.

3   Remove the wire from the pliers. Grip the eye in the jaws of flat-nose pliers and place the crossed looped end into the jaws of round-nose or chain-nose pliers.

4   Wrap the short length of wire around the main body of the wire as close to the eye as possible. Keep the wraps neatly together as you move down the wire.

5   After two or three wraps snip off the end of the wrapping wire as close to the last coil as possible. File the end of the cut wire to smooth the end.

6   Repeat the steps to make another wrapped loop at the end of the bead. Then trim off the excess wire using wire snips.

knots

In many different cultures and countries, the craft of knot tying has been passed down through the ages. The Japanese, for example, have used knots for centuries. Many of their traditional knots symbolize love, happiness, good health, even death. Celtic knots are also famous throughout the world, especially for jewellery making.

MACRAMÉ KNOTS

There are many different macramé knots that can be created with either twine, raffia, silk, leather or synthetic cords. The thinner the cord the finer and smaller the knot will appear. The two macramé knots used in this book are the lark's head and the square knot, which are both very versatile. These can be used to make endless bracelets and can be further enhanced with the addition of beads.

LARK'S HEAD KNOT

This is an anchoring knot used at the start of a piece for many of the macramé knots.

1   Cut a length of cord. (For practising it needs to be 39in [100cm] in length.)

2   Fold the cord in half, then take the fold and thread it through the ring.

3   Pass the free ends of the cord through the loop of the cord and pull them down firmly to form the knot.

SQUARE KNOT

A lark's head knot is required at the start of a square knot. It may help to hang the ring you are using at the start of the knot on a hook so that you can use both hands.

Practise these knots on scraps of cord until you are comfortable with the interweaving of the cords. The first time, colour one cord red and the other green to help you visually with the knotting process.

1 Having made a lark's head knot, lay it down making sure that the knot is facing towards you. Take the right-hand cord (red) and lay it over the left-hand cord (green). Pick up the red cord and pass it over and under the green cord. Pull both cords so that they slide up against the lark's head knot.

2 Pass the green cord back over the red cord, leaving it a little slack. Take the red cord and pass it over and under the green cord. Pull the cords gently until they slide up against the start of the knot that was made in the first step. This will make a square knot. Repeat both steps to make additional knots.

OVERHAND KNOT

This simple knot will hold particularly well, especially when painted with nail varnish once it's tied.

1 With an overhand knot the aim is to get the knot as tight as possible against the beads so that the elastic cord doesn't show through. If the knot is chunky, once tied it can be covered with a ribbon or charm.

2 Line up the two ends of the elastic, making sure that they are both the same length. If they are uneven, slide some of the beads along the cord until they are even. Stretch the cords out while holding the beads in place with your other hand.

3 Loop the two ends of the elastic cord around the pointer finger of the other hand and pass the ends through the loop. Slip your finger out, pulling the knot tight up against the beads.

4 Tie a second knot as close to the first as possible. Paint the knot with nail varnish before snipping off the excess cord. Pull the knot back through the closest bead to hide it.

Techniques

clasps

Clasps are the closure finding used to complete bracelets and necklaces. Attaching them to your finished piece is easy, and making your own clasps will give your work a designer finish.

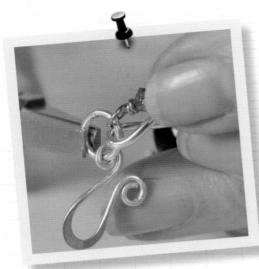

SIMPLE SILVER CLASP

This handmade clasp adds a designer's touch to a simple bracelet and can be made in just a few minutes (see page 25 for details on how to make them). Practise with base metal, then when you have mastered the technique move onto fine or sterling silver to create something extra special. Experiment with various thicknesses and sizes that can be used in future projects.

ATTACHING CLASPS

1   Open a strong jumpring with flat-nose or chain-nose pliers. It should be thin enough to pass through the round link on the clasp.

2   Slide the jumpring into the last link on the end of the bracelet as well as the round link on the end of the clasp. Close the ring, bringing the ends of the bracelet and the clasp together securely.

3   Toggle clasps have a bar to close the clasp. Use steps 1 and 2 to attach the clasp and the toggle to each end of the bracelet.

MAKING A SIMPLE SILVER CLASP

1 Measure and cut off a length of wire approximately 2¾in (7cm) long. With the very point of the round-nose pliers grip one end of the wire and twist it into a tiny loop.

2 Grip the edge of the wire loop in the jaws of the chain-nose pliers. Use the index finger of your dominant hand to bend the wire gently towards the pliers.

3 Bend the wire into a soft loop so that the free end just touches and lies parallel with the coiled end. Make another little loop in the end of the wire with round-nose pliers.

4 With your fingers, hold the soft loop of the clasp firmly on the steel block. Hammer the loop gently on one side, turn it over, then hammer the other side.

5 Repeat this action until the loop flattens out slightly. It should take on an attractive flat shape.

6 Gently sand the wire using the sanding pad (280 grade) to remove any scratches in the metal. Do this using a circular motion so as not to scratch the metal any further. The clasp is now ready to be attached to your bracelet with jumprings.

materials
- Round-nose pliers
- Chain-nose or flat-nose pliers
- Hammer
- Steel block
- Silver or copper wire
- Sanding pad (280 grade)

SILVER CLASPS

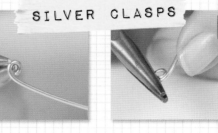

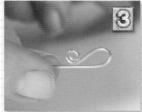

IF YOU ARE USING FINE SILVER TO CREATE A MORE EXPENSIVE LOOK, MELT THE ENDS OF THE WIRE BEFORE COILING, AS YOU WOULD IF MAKING HEADPINS. SEE PAGE 20 FOR MORE DETAILS.

Techniques

drilling

It's not difficult to make a hole in an object to attach it to a jumpring. A basic hand drill will do the job effectively. They are also inexpensive and easily available at hardware stores. Purchase several fine drill bits that will fit the gauge of wire or size of jumpring you wish to link to the hole.

1   Fit the drill into the part of the clamp that grips the drill to the base of the tool, then tighten it. Tape the item you wish to make a hole in to a wooden board. Mark on the tape with pencil or pen exactly where you wish to drill.

2   Postion the drill on top of the mark you have made. Holding it vertically, turn the handle forwards so that the drill begins to bite into the metal. As you work, apply a little pressure to help the drill cut in.

3   When the drill has gone right through, carefully reverse the action of the handle and remove the drill.

DON'T FORGET!

BEFORE USING THE DRILL, MAKE SURE THAT YOU READ THE INSTRUCTIONS ABOUT ATTACHING AND RELEASING THE DRILL BIT CAREFULLY.

hammering

Silversmith hammers are used to flatten, add texture and to change the shape of wire or metal, whether on solid metal mandrels or rods. A flat steel block is ideal for texturing metal shapes, as well as making clasps or findings.

1   Cut the wire to the desired length. Shape the ends with round-nose pliers. Curve your piece into the shape you wish to make, then place it onto the steel block.

2   Hammer one side with the head of the hammer, before turning the piece over and hammering the other side. This action will flatten the metal, harden it and ensure that it remains flat. Hammering only one side may cause the piece to warp.

3   The end of the hammer can be used to create patterns on the metal. A hammer with a ball end is used to shape and dome metal. The chisel end on a hammer will form indents on the metal and distress it. Experiment on scraps of wire or metal before working on your prepared piece.

Techniques

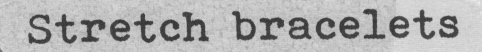

Stretch bracelets

florence

Glass floral hearts strung with faceted red beads

Everything you'll need...

Florence is one of the most romantic cities in the world, as well as the heart of glass beads and sculpture work. This delightful heart bracelet will put a sparkle in your eyes and a mischievous smile on your lips.

1

4  × 20

3 × 8

2

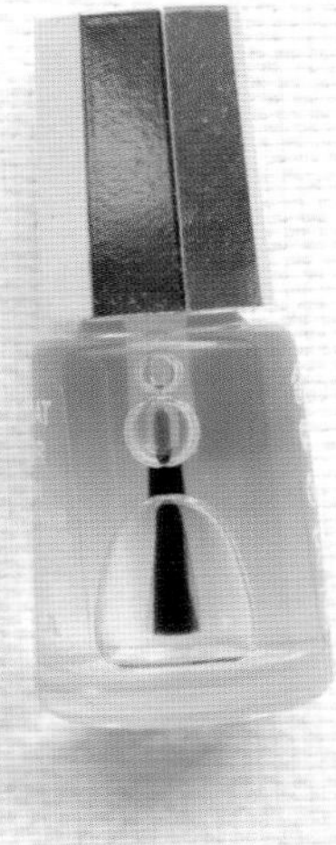

5

1 Tape measure
2 Stretch illusion cord
3 8 x ⁹/₁₆in (15mm) long heart beads
4 20 x ⁵/₃₂in (4mm) faceted glass beads
5 Clear nail varnish

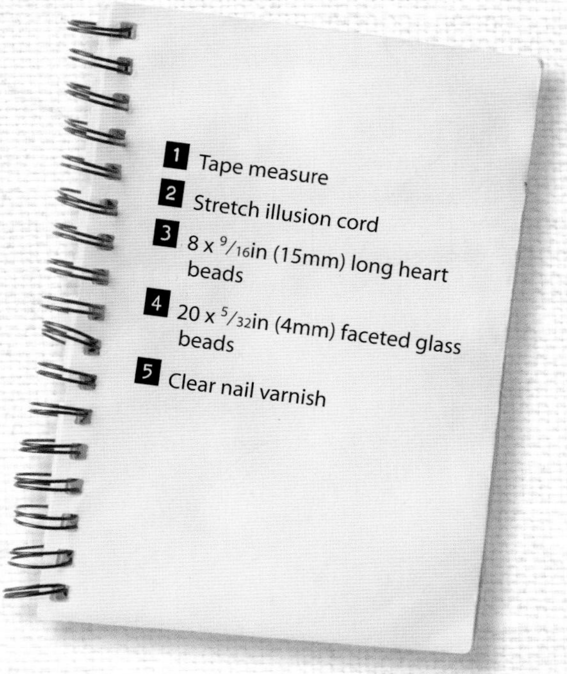

Assembling florence

1 Wrap a length of elastic around your wrist, being careful not to stretch it. Add another ⁹/₁₆in (15mm) to this length, so you have enough to make a knot. If you are using relatively heavy beads, use two or three strands of elastic for additional strength.

2 Thread a ⁵/₃₂in (4mm) bead onto the elastic, making a small knot at one end to hold it in place. This stopper bead will prevent the other beads from sliding off.

3 Continue to thread on three more ⁵/₃₂in (4mm) beads.

4 Follow these beads with a heart bead, bearing in mind the direction that the bead is facing. To recreate the illustrated bracelet, pass the elastic through the base of the bead and out of the heart shape at the top.

5 Thread on a ⁵/₃₂in (4mm) bead followed by another heart bead. This time, pass the elastic through the top of the bead and out through the base. Repeat this pattern from step 2 until all the beads have been used.

6 Carefully untie the stopper bead, holding onto both ends of the elastic. Tie the ends together with a simple or overhand knot (see page 23).

7 Paint clear nail varnish over the knot to secure it. Do not use glue as this may cause the elastic to perish. Finally, use scissors to cut off the ends of the elastic.

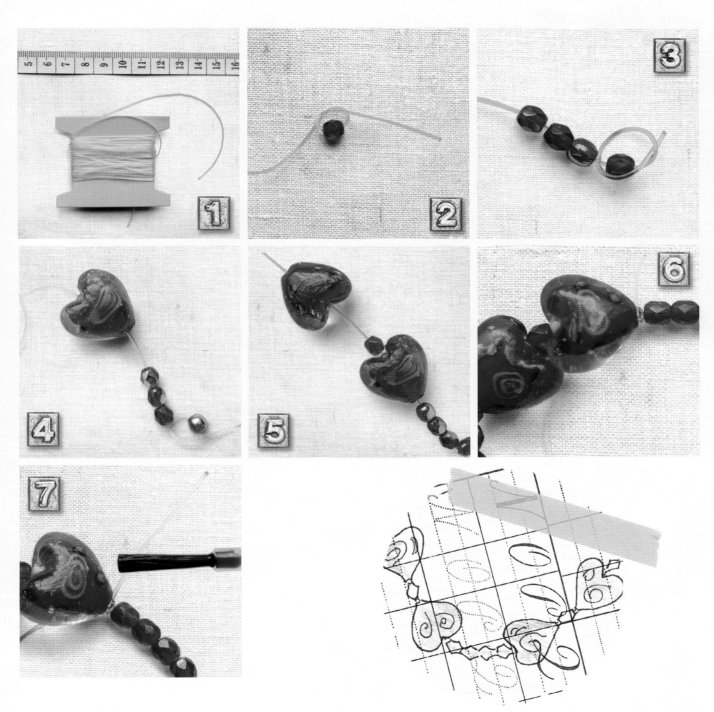

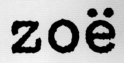

zoë

Use a variety of different coloured
beads to create a sparkling rainbow

Everything you'll need...

This silver charm bracelet is deceptively easy to put together. Make it today to wear tonight. Heads will turn as you flash this little sparkler.

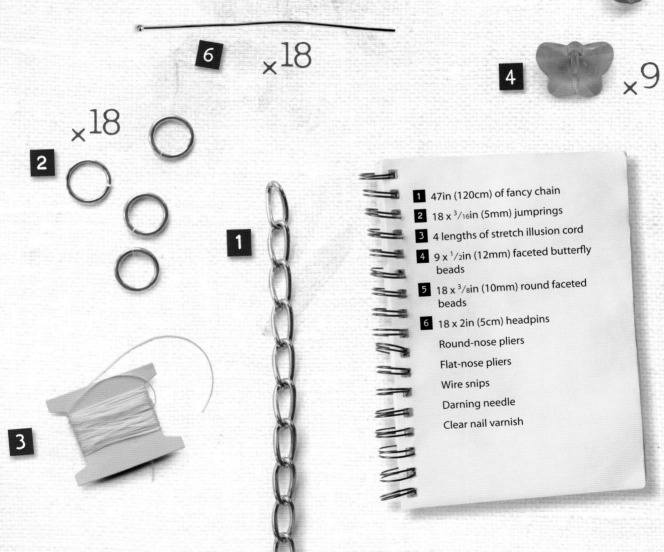

1. 47in (120cm) of fancy chain
2. 18 x $^{3}/_{16}$in (5mm) jumprings
3. 4 lengths of stretch illusion cord
4. 9 x $^{1}/_{2}$in (12mm) faceted butterfly beads
5. 18 x $^{3}/_{8}$in (10mm) round faceted beads
6. 18 x 2in (5cm) headpins

Round-nose pliers

Flat-nose pliers

Wire snips

Darning needle

Clear nail varnish

Assembling zoë

1 Attach 18 jumprings at regular intervals to links in a chain around 47in (120cm) in length. The distance between each one does not have to be exact, but even spaces do look better.

2 Measure your wrist, then add on a further 12in (30cm). Cut four strands of stretch illusion cord to this length. Tie one end of the four strands to a link in the chain using an overhand knot (see page 23).

3 Thread all four strands through the eye of a darning needle.

4 Weave the needle in and out of every second link in the chain. This is not difficult, but it can be time-consuming, yet an even weave gives the best results.

5 To make the beaded charms, create simple eyepins at the end of each headpin just above the bead. Or you can wire wrap the pins to make them more secure. The butterfly beads here show a simple eye finished at the end of the headpins by using round-nose pliers (see page 18).

To create the double-beaded charms, thread two beads onto a headpin, then make a wrapped loop or a simple eye at the end of the pin to secure them into place.

6 Attach the butterfly and beaded charms to the jumprings on the chain.

7 When you reach the end of the chain, undo the knot used to fasten the strands of cord and pull the elastic tight to fit your wrist. Keeping it tight, tie all eight strands together with an overhand slip knot (see page 23), then cover the knot with nail varnish. Once it has dried, snip off the ends of the cord with scissors.

sunny

The fun part is watching the
beads interlock when you tie the knot

Everything you'll need...

These brightly coloured, funky, interlocking beads are fun to work with and can be used to create unusual and quirky bracelets.

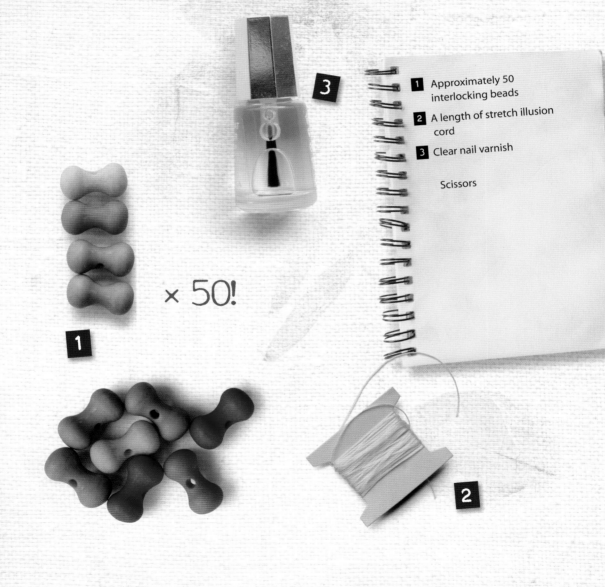

3

1 Approximately 50 interlocking beads

2 A length of stretch illusion cord

3 Clear nail varnish

Scissors

× 50!

1

2

Assembling sunny

1 Measure your wrist, adding a further 12in (30cm). Cut a length of stretch illusion cord to this length.

2 Lay the beads out, ideally on a non-slip work mat. Arrange them to create a pleasing colour palette by using beads of alternate colours, or mix them up for a more random look.

3 Thread the beads onto the stretch illusion cord so that they lie in a straight line. Do not pull the cord until all the beads have been added.

4 When you have used all the beads, pull the cord so that they all fall into one another. Tie the bracelet around your wrist to be sure that it fits snugly. Add or subtract beads to suit.

5 Tie an overhand knot close to the end beads (see page 23). Then, tie a second knot close to the first.

6 Paint both knots with clear nail varnish to seal them. When the varnish is dry, snip the cord close to the knots. Slide the knots into the hole of one of the end beads to hide the join.

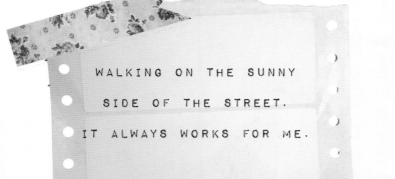

WALKING ON THE SUNNY
SIDE OF THE STREET.
IT ALWAYS WORKS FOR ME.

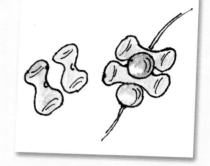

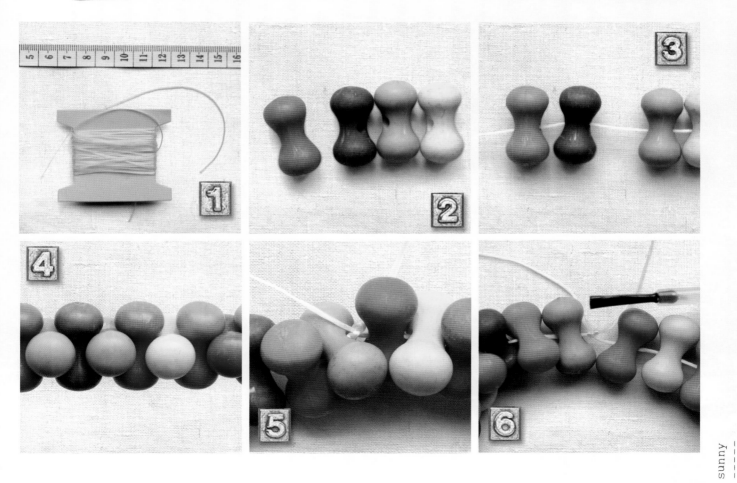

pepper

These beads look like
licorice allsorts, but
are calorie-free!

Everything you'll need...

Say it as it is! Alphabet beads are a great way to speak your mind and, at the same time, add a touch of humour.

1 2 lengths of stretch illusion cord

2 10 x ¹⁄₄in (6mm) cube beads

3 13 alphabet beads (will vary depending on your message)

4 3 x ³⁄₈in (10mm) round beads

5 13 small silver spacer beads

6 Silver split ring

7 Heart watch face

8 Small scrap of ribbon

Scissors

Clear nail varnish

pepper

Assembling pepper

1 Measure your wrist, adding a further 15½in (40cm). Cut two lengths of stretch illusion cord to match this measurement. Make a loose knot in one end of the cords so that the beads will not slip off.

2 Lay out the alphabet beads, ideally on a non-slip mat, and use them to write your message. It could be an inspiring thought, a cheeky comment or simply the name of your loved one.

3 Mix and match the beads and spacers to form an attractive pattern. Place silver spacers between the beads to add definition.

4 Thread the two strands of stretch illusion cord through the alphabet beads. Check that all the beads are facing in the same direction.

5 Untie the end knot in the stretch illusion cord. Hold the ends of the cord firmly against the end beads as you tie an overhand knot (see page 23). Dot a little clear nail varnish on the knot to secure it. Once it is dry, snip off the ends with scissors.

6 Open a split ring using the split ring pliers. Slide the heart watch face onto the split ring and thread it through until the spring clips close. Attach the ring to the bracelet and finish by tying a ribbon over the knotted cord.

Stringing

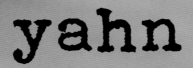

yahn

This bracelet exudes oriental charm
with a sophisticated, casual appeal

Everything you'll need...

While on your travels, collect beads from the places you visit. String these together and create a memory bracelet to remind you of your fabulous adventures.

5

×9

1

×2

2 **×12**

4

3 **×2**

1 2 x ⁵/₁₆in (8mm) jumprings

2 12 small silver spacer beads
(more for a larger bracelet)

3 2 x ¼in (6mm) silver beetle beads

4 Silver magnetic clasp

5 Oriental beads
2 x ³/₈in (10mm), 2 x ½in (12mm),
2 x ⁹/₁₆in (15mm), 2 x ¹³/₁₆in (20mm),
1 x 1in (25mm)

2 silver crimps

2 silver calottes

Silver-coated nylon stringing thread

Epoxy glue

Round-nose, chain-nose and flat-nose pliers

yahn

Assembling yahn

1 Cut off approximately 12in (30cm) of nylon stringing thread. Place a crimp onto the end of the thread. Create a small loop, then crimp the bead as near to the top of this loop as possible.

2 Slide the other end of the thread through the hole at the base of the calotte. Pass all the thread through the hole, ensuring that the crimped end is neatly pulled into the base of the calotte. Place a tiny drop of glue onto the end of the crimp, then close the calotte using chain-nose pliers.

3 Thread a few hand-painted oriental beads onto the thread separated by small silver spacer beads and beetle beads. The pattern shown here is created using a variety of different-sized beads. The largest bead is in the centre of the pattern.

4 As you work, try the bracelet on your wrist for size. Handmade beads tend to be irregular in size, so don't worry if they don't match perfectly. At the end of the bracelet, slide a calotte onto the end of the thread.

5 Slide a final crimp onto the end of the thread. Make a small loop by passing the free end of the thread through the crimp. Carefully pull the thread down until it sits flush with the inside of the calotte. Crimp the bead and trim off any excess thread. Then use chain-nose pliers to close the calotte.

6 Use flat-nose pliers to attach jump-rings to both ends of the magnetic clasps. Finally, link the ends of the calottes to the jumprings using chain-nose pliers.

TO PROTECT CERAMIC BEADS, STORE THEM IN A SOFT FABRIC OR VELVET POUCH.

rose

Using bead caps adds a touch
of glamour to plain beads

Everything you'll need...

Create pieces of dramatic jewellery with richly coloured beads and silver Aztec spacers. Opt for large beads, textured metal and unusual focal pieces to create maximum impact.

×4

2

8

×4

5

6

7

1

3

×2

×8

4

1 4 x ³⁄₄in (18mm) Aztec silver beads

2 4 x ¹³⁄₁₆in (20mm) purple acrylic beads

3 2 x ¹⁄₄in (6mm) Aztec silver beads

4 8 bead caps

5 A purple acrylic rose

6 1 x ⁵⁄₁₆in (8mm) jumpring

7 1 x ³⁄₈in (10mm) jumpring

8 A parrot clasp

2 silver crimps

Flat-nose pliers

Wire snips

Nylon-coated silver

rose

Assembling rose

1 Cut a length of silver-coated nylon thread to fit your wrist. Add an extra 6in (15cm) to this length to allow room for the crimped loops. Create a small loop at one end of the thread and crimp it securely (see page 14).

2 Link an open ⁵⁄₁₆in (8mm) jumpring to this loop, then attach it to the base of the silver clasp. Close the jumpring using the flat-nose pliers (see page 16).

3 Slide a bead cap onto the thread and up close to the crimped loop. Add a purple bead followed by another silver bead cap. The bead caps should cover each end of the bead.

4 Add an Aztec spacer, then another bead cap, followed by a purple bead and another bead cap. Lastly, slide on a second Aztec spacer.

5 Follow the last spacer with a ¼in (6mm) floral bead spacer, an acrylic purple rose and another floral bead spacer.

6 Reverse the pattern, then finish the bracelet with a crimped loop. Attach a ³⁄₈in (10mm) jumpring to the end.

IF YOU HAVE A LARGE WRIST ADD MORE BEADS AS YOU WORK. USE A LONGER LENGTH OF THREAD AND SIMPLIFY.

rose

pearl

A combination of pretty shells
and pearls

Everything you'll need...

Make your own designer-style jewellery with macramé knots. This simple knotting method is used to make fine, tactile jewellery and with a little practice is easy to master.

4

7 × 4

× 3

2

× 4

3

1   4 coin charms

2   3 shells

3   4 pearl drops

4   Clasp with jumprings attached

5   A ribbon crimp

6   A split ring

7   4 x 2in (5cm) headpins

     Round-nose, flat-nose and chain-nose pliers

     Clear nail varnish

     39in (100cm) memory wire cord

     4 x 5/16in (8mm) jumprings

× 4

1

5

6

Assembling pearl

1 Fold the cord in half and thread the fold through the coin opening. Pass the ends of the cord through the loop, pulling them down firmly to form a lark's head knot (see page 22).

2 Lay the cords in front of you. Take the right-hand cord over the top of the left-hand one to create a loop. Move the left-hand cord up and under the loop. Pull the cords tightly together to create the start of a square knot.

3 Next, lay the left-hand cord over the right. Pass the right-hand cord over and then under the left. Pull the cords tightly together to form a square knot (see page 23).

4 Repeat steps 2 and 3 until you have made three square knots.

5 Pass the ends of the cord through the holes at the top of the shell. Check that the shell is hanging down in the direction that the pearl drops are to be hung from the coins.

6 Make another three square knots, then pass the two ends of the cords under a coin and up through the square hole in the centre. Separate the cords where they formed the last knot and pass the ends of the cord through the hole, pulling them firmly into place.

7 Pass the cords behind the coin and through the hole in the centre from the other side. Pull both cords tight with the top cord pulled upwards.

8 Continue the pattern of knots, adding more shells and coins until the bracelet fits your wrist. Attach a final coin and create a square knot. Place pearl drops onto headpins and wire wrap them securely. Using jumprings, attach the drops to the coins.

9 Cut the cord, paint it with nail varnish and crimp the knot using a ribbon crimp. Finally, attach the clasp to the ends of the bracelet using jumprings.

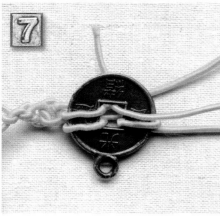

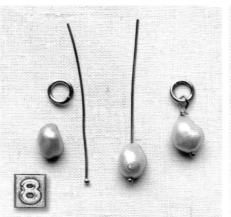

pebbles

For maximum impact, match your shoes and bag with this bracelet

Everything you'll need...

Strand these glittering beads and colourful pebbles together to create a bracelet packed with glamour and style. A striking accessory for that little black dress.

3 × 14–16

6 × 4

7

1

2 × 2

× 4

5

4

× 3

1 Silver tiger tail

2 2 diamanté spacers

3 14–16 x 5/16in (8mm) crystal beads (the number will depend on your wrist size)

4 4 silver pebbles

5 3 pink pebbles

6 4 split rings

7 Toggle clasp with double eyes

4 silver crimps

Crimping and split ring pliers

Scissors

Assembling pebbles

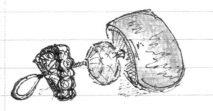

1 Cut two lengths of tiger tail to fit your wrist, adding a further 6in (15cm) to this measurement. Thread a crimp onto one end of each length. Make a small loop and crimp the loops securely.

2 Thread one free end of the tiger tail through the top hole of the diamanté spacer. Pull the thread through until the crimp sits up against the hole.

3 Onto both threads of tiger tail, thread a faceted bead followed by a pebble. Continue this pattern until all the beads and pebbles have been used, then end with a crystal.

4 Thread the ends of the tiger tail through a second diamanté spacer and finish it off with crimped loops.

5 Attach split rings to the eyes on the toggle and the clasp, taking great care when separating the coils in the split ring (see page 17).

6 Finally, use the split ring pliers to reopen the split rings. Slide on the loops of tiger tail that are extending from the ends of the diamanté spacers.

FACETED BEADS HAVE BOTH A MIRRORED AND A FACETED SIDE TO REFLECT THE LIGHT.

THIS GIVES AN ADDITIONAL SPARKLE TO THE BRACELET TO MAKE IT EXTRA SPECIAL.

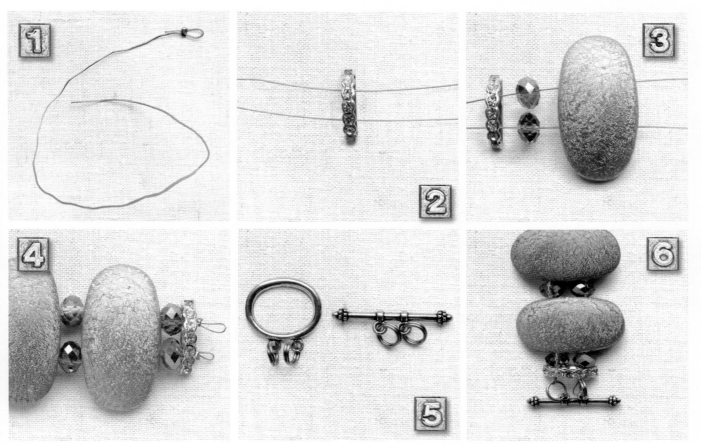

linking

minni

Cheerful, cheeky charms

Everything you'll need...

When cats and mice come out to play, there's sure to be some fun and games. These cheeky beads will certainly raise a smile.

2 ×3

5 ×4

6

3 ×3

4 ×5

1. A length of fancy link chain
2. 3 glass mouse beads
3. 3 glass cat beads
4. 5 x $5/16$in (8mm) jumprings
5. 4 x $5/32$in (4mm) crystal beads
6. A clasp

6 x $3/16$in (5mm) jumprings

4 x 2in (5cm) headpins

Wire snips

Round-nose, flat-nose and chain-nose pliers

1

minni

Assembling minni

1 Cut a length of chain long enough to fit around your wrist. Attach 6 x ³/₁₆in (5mm) jumprings to the links at regular intervals.

2 Using flat and chain-nose pliers, attach a ⁵/₁₆in (8mm) jumpring to each end of the chain (see page 16). Attach a ⁵/₁₆in (8mm) jumpring to the glass loop at the top of each mouse bead.

3 Leave the jumprings open and link them to the ³/₁₆in (5mm) rings you have already attached to the chain, then close the jumprings to fix the beads in place.

4 Thread the cat beads onto headpins and make wire-wrapped loops at the head of each bead (see page 21). Attach these beads to the remaining ³/₁₆in (5mm) jumprings that are already linked to the chain.

5 To create the small beaded headpin, simply thread four little crystal beads onto a headpin. Make a wrapped loop and link the loop to one of the ⁵/₁₆in (8mm) jumprings at the end of the chain. Use matching beads or a mix of different ones.

6 To finish, attach the clasp to the bracelet using toggle clasps, parrot clasps or a handmade clasp.

shelly

Link these discs together for a colourful piece

Everything you'll need...

Stitching pearl buttons onto your clothing can create an instant new look. When updating your wardrobe why not make some matching snazzy bracelets?

2

×9

1

3

4

5

1 Half-hard wire in 10 x ³/₃₂in (2.5mm) lengths

2 9 x ¹³/₁₆in (20mm) wide shell discs (more for a larger wrist)

3 Parrot clasp with jumpring attached

4 1³/₁₆in (30mm) fine fancy chain

5 Headpin with 1 x ⁵/₃₂in (4mm) faceted bead

Wire snips

Round-nose and chain-nose pliers

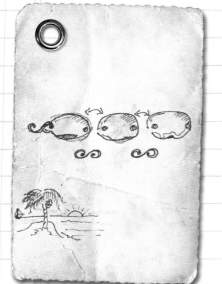

Assembling shelly

1 Use half-hard wire to make the links. Hold one end of the wire in round-nose pliers and roll the wire into a neat loop. Repeat this action on the opposite side, but this time turn the loop in the opposite direction. To gain even-sized loops, use the same position on the pliers' jaws when making each loop.

2 Measure your wrist, then add on a further $^{13}/_{16}$in (20mm). Either select shells of the same colour or mix and match pretty shades and arrange them in a pattern that stretches to the length of your wrist.

3 Using the chain-nose pliers, open the loops at each end of the links very slightly. Slip the shell discs onto each loop, then carefully close them with the pliers.

4 When you have connected a chain of shells, attach a parrot clasp to one end using the jumpring attached to the clasp. Link this with the last link on a shell disc.

5 Finally, attach a small length of chain to the remaining end link using chain-nose pliers. Thread a small crystal onto a headpin, create a simple eye and link this to the end of the chain.

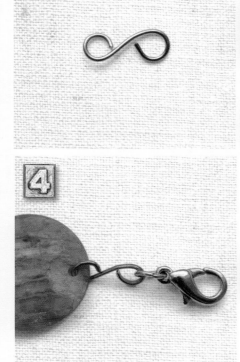

THE WELL-KNOWN TONGUE TWISTER
'SHE SELLS SEA SHELLS BESIDE THE SEASHORE'
INSPIRED THIS SHELL DESIGN.

shelly
- - - - -

mille

Unique charms evoke positive emotions

Everything you'll need...

Millefiori is a combination of two Italian words, *mille* (thousand) and *fiori* (flowers). With their bright, and vibrant colours, these beads are perfect for this bright emotive bracelet!

5 × 6

6 × 7

1 × 7

2 × 7

3

× 6

4

1   7 x 2in (5cm) eyepins

2   7 x ⁹/₁₆in (15mm) millefiori beads (more for a larger wrist)

3   6 charms

4   Parrot clasp with jumpring attached

5   6 x ³/₈in (10mm) jumprings

6   7 x ³/₁₆in (5mm) jumprings

  Round-nose and chain-nose pliers

  Wire cutters

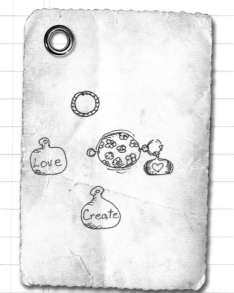

Assembling mille

1 Select the millefiori beads you wish to use in your bracelet.

2 Thread an eyepin through each bead. Make a 90-degree bend on the eyeless piece of wire that juts out.

3 Snip off all but ¼in (6mm) of the wire eyepin. Grip the end of the pin in round-nose pliers to make another eye in the wire (see page 18).

4 Attach ³/₁₆in (5mm) jumprings to each of the charms, then close them. Those used in the illustrated bracelet are double-sided with a symbol that matches the text.

5 Open all the ³/₈in (10mm) jumprings. Link a millefiori bead to each one, then a charm, followed by another linked bead. Close the jumprings securely.

6 Continue to link all the beads and charms together in a chain. Finish the bracelet off with a millefiori bead.

7 Using the small jumpring that is already attached to the parrot clasp, fasten the clasp to an eye on the end of one of the last millefiori beads. Finish off by attaching a jumpring to the remaining eye and clipping the whole bracelet closed.

annie

These pebbles are as
light as a feather

Everything you'll need...

Lava rock pebbles combined with coiled wire links create a very feminine piece with a modern edge. Hammering the wire coils is also a great stress-busting activity!

1 × 3

3 × 2

5

2 × 2

6

4 × 6

1 3 lava pebbles (more for a larger wrist)

39in x $\frac{1}{64}$in (100cm x 0.5mm) fine silver wire

2 12in x $\frac{1}{32}$in (30cm x 0.08mm) silver plated copper wire

3 2 x $\frac{3}{16}$in (5mm) glass beads

4 6 x $\frac{5}{16}$in (8mm) jumprings

5 Magnetic clasp with jumprings attached

6 Short length of fancy silver chain

Round-nose, flat-nose and chain-nose pliers

Assembling annie

1 Cut two lengths of ¹/₃₂in (0.08mm) wire to a length of 4in (10cm). Make a tiny coil at one end using the point of the round-nose pliers. Grip the coil in the jaws of the flat-nose pliers and make three tight coils. Repeat this action at the other end of the wire to make two coiled links going in the opposite direction.

2 Place a wire coil on a steel block and hammer the coil to flatten it out. Once both ends have been hammered, turn the coil over and flatten the opposite side. Hammer the second coil, then bend the coils slightly in the centre so that they curve around your wrist.

3 Cut off a 3¹/₄in (8cm) length of ¹/₆₄in (0.5mm) wire and make a wrapped loop at one end. Thread the end of the wire under the coiled link and up through the hole in its centre. Next, slide a blue bead onto the wire.

4 Pass the wire back down through the hole in the other coil. Pull the wire tight until the bead sits on the coil link. Make another wrapped loop at the end of the wire. Repeat steps 3 and 4 to decorate the second coiled loop.

5 Cut three 3¹/₄in (8cm) lengths of ¹/₆₄in (0.5mm) wire. Then make a wrapped loop at one end of a piece of wire. Pass the free end through one of the lava pebbles and secure it with another wrapped loop. Link the pebble to the coiled link using a ⁵/₁₆in (8mm) jumpring. Repeat this step for all the pebbles, linking each one to the coils.

6 To finish, cut the chain in half and link it to the magnetic clasp with jumprings. Attach the free ends of the chain to the remaining wrapped loops that extend from the three lava pebbles.

recycled

joules

Forgotten jewels create new treasures

Everything you'll need...

Raid your jewellery box for broken necklaces to make into unique bracelets.

1

×2

3

2

×2

4

1. Old broken necklace
2. 2 split rings
3. 2 parrot clasps with jumprings attached
4. Small length of chain

Wire snips split ring, flat- nose and chain-nose pliers

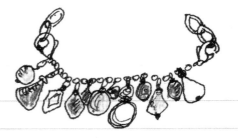

Assembling joules

1 Charity shops are the perfect place to rummage for old necklaces that can easily be revamped. Choose a piece with lots of pretty beads on. Cut the necklace in half and store the excess pieces.

2 Using split ring pliers, carefully open a split ring and slide it onto one end of the chain that the beads are linked to. Twist the split ring until it is securely on the chain link. Add the remaining split ring to the other end of the chain.

3 Open the split rings again with the pliers and attach a silver parrot clasp to each ring. Measure your wrist with a tape measure, then add $1^{3}/_{16}$in (30mm) to this measurement.

4 Lay the beaded chain with the clasps against the tape measure to find out how much chain you will need to finish the bracelet.

5 Cut the required length of chain and clip the clasps to the ends of the chain links. If the links are too small, you can use jumprings to attach the chain.

THIS BRACELET CAN BE
UNCLIPPED FROM THE CHAIN
AND WORN AS A NECKLACE.

miss jane

Step back in time

Everything you'll need...

Deconstruct an old watch and use the parts to create imaginative, steampunk-inspired pieces.

1 Short length of fancy chain

2 Old watch face

3 Key charm

4 Metal watch cog

5 Small timepiece

6 Metal washer

7 Parrot clasp

8 4 x $^5/_{16}$in (8mm) jumprings or split rings

Epoxy glue (quick dry)

Old paintbrush

Round-nose and flat-nose pliers

miss jane

Assembling miss jane

1 Mix the two-part epoxy glue together. Be sure to use equal parts or the glue will not set. Place a small amount onto the back of the watch cog using an old paint brush. Press jumprings into the glue on either side of the cog, before leaving it to dry.

2 Once the jumprings have set, lay the pieces out and work out your pattern before gluing them together. Here the washer has been glued onto the top of the cog followed by the clock face and finished with a small charm. Allow the glue to dry before handling the piece, as it may smudge and spoil the parts.

3 Attach a jumpring to one of the other jumprings already attached to the cog. Use chain-nose and flat-nose pliers to secure it firmly to the chain.

4 Use another jumpring to attach an additional time piece or charm onto the chain, securing it into place using pliers.

5 Link this jumpring to the end of the parrot clasp and close it with the pliers. To fasten the bracelet, clip the clasp to the free jumpring that is glued to the back of the watch cog.

Steampunk is much more than simply a combination of brass and watchparts. It combines the past and the future in an aesthetically pleasing and modern way.

THIS BRACELET IS BASED ON THE STORY OF AN ADVENTURESS WHO TIME-TRAVELLED INTO THE AGE OF STEAM. HER MAGICAL KEY DISGUISED AS A WATCH OPENED A PORTAL INTO THE MYSTERIOUS PAST.

amy

Transform your treasures

Everything you'll need...

Even odds and ends can be useful. Make good use of old chains or earrings that have lost their pair.

6

1

2

3

×2

×4

4

×6

5

1 Short lengths of chain with clasp attached

2 6 jumprings or split rings

3 2 crystals

4 4 small charms

5 An earring

6 Fine wire

Split ring, chain-nose and flat-nose pliers

Assembling amy

1 Using split ring pliers, link a split ring to the top of the earring. Slide the split ring until it is securely attached to the earring.

2 Thread wire through the crystals and make a wrapped loop at the head of each one (see page 21).

3 Attach the charms and crystals onto the lengths of chain with split rings or jumprings (see page 16–17).

4 To make a cluster of charms, open a large jumpring and thread on several small charms. Close the jumpring with the chain-nose and flat-nose pliers.

5 Attach the earring to the chain using split rings. Lay out the bracelet as you work and continue to link the sections together until you are happy with the finished piece.

THIS LOVELY EARRING WAS A GIFT
FROM MY HUSBAND, BUT UNFORTUNATELY
I LOST ITS PARTNER. BY LINKING IT
ONTO THIS SECONDHAND CHAIN I CAN
NOW WEAR IT AGAIN AND ENJOY THE
MEMORIES ATTACHED TO IT.

amy

jan

Charm and elegance combined

Everything you'll need...

Add a fancy clasp onto a small piece of an enamel necklace and link it with a leather cord to create a fabulous bracelet.

×2

1. Enamel and crystal necklace
2. Yellow leather cord
3. Copper clasp
4. 2 jumprings
5. Fine copper wire
6. Ribbon crimp

Flat-nose and chain-nose pliers

Clippers

Assembling jan

1 Lay out the necklace to decide which piece would work best for making the bracelet. Make sure that this piece has ends that can be linked to jumprings. Clip off the section you have chosen using wire clippers. Keep the clippers sharp by snipping sandpaper a few times. The glass grit will help to keep the clippers in top condition.

2 Measure your wrist and add 1³/₁₆in (30mm) to the length. Lay the piece on the tape measure to calculate how much leather cord is needed. Cut a piece of cord twice the required length. Then cut a chain half as long.

3 Fold the cord in half, then crimp the cut ends together with a ribbon crimp (see page 15). Link the wire-wrapped end of cord to the clasp toggle with a jumpring. Attach the chain to the same jumpring, then use chain-nose and flat-nose pliers to close it securely.

4 To create a neat loop at the other end of the cord, squeeze the two lengths together and firmly wrap them a large crimp bead or fine copper wire (snip off the excess wire with clippers). Link this end to one end of the jewellery piece and to the other end of the chain with another jumpring.

5 Attach a clasp to the other end of the bracelet with the remaining jumpring.

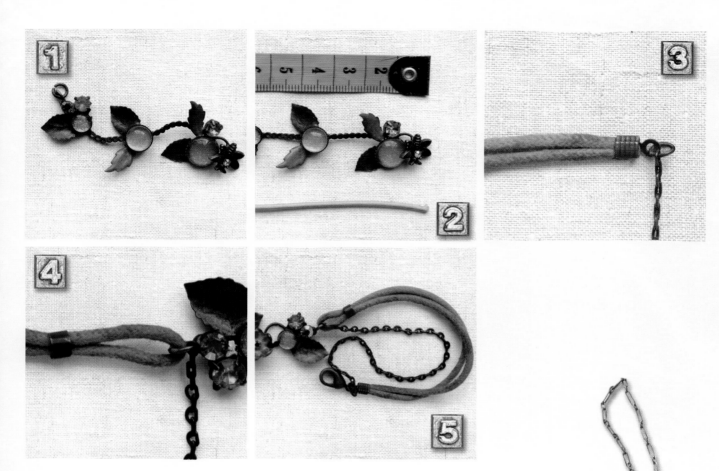

SAVE ANY EXTRA PIECES TO MAKE
EARRINGS AND A MATCHING NECKLACE.
STORE THEM IN A SMALL ORGANZA
BAG TO KEEP THEM SAFE.

My sister and I used to sit in the grass all summer long, making daisy chains in the sunshine.

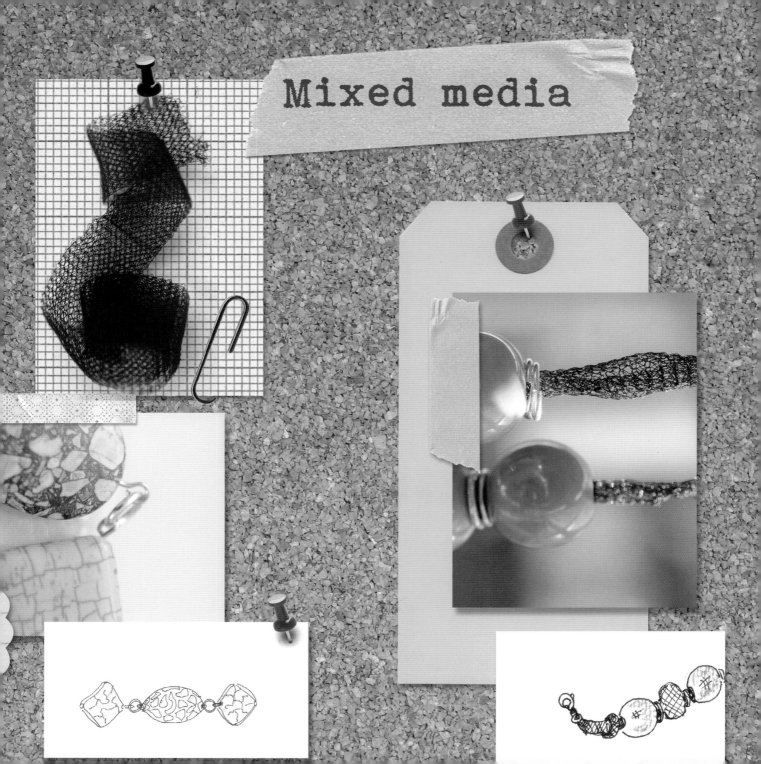

Mixed media

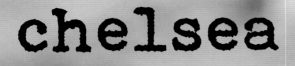

chelsea

Bold and beautiful

Everything you'll need...

Think outside the square. Use knitted tubes of wire to link ceramic beads. Their glassy glaze catches the light, making this the perfect bead for an evening bracelet.

× 6

× 10

5

3

2

4

1

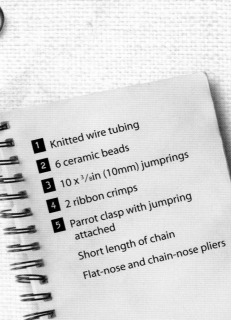

1 Knitted wire tubing

2 6 ceramic beads

3 10 x ³/₈in (10mm) jumprings

4 2 ribbon crimps

5 Parrot clasp with jumpring attached

Short length of chain

Flat-nose and chain-nose pliers

chelsea

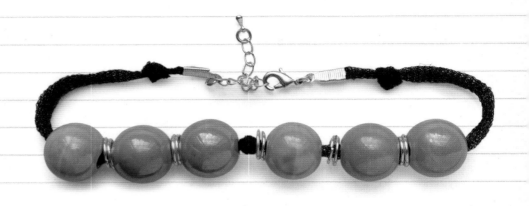

Assembling chelsea

1 Measure a length of knitted wire to fit your wrist, adding on an additional 2³⁄₄in (7cm) before cutting.

2 Tie a knot in the end of the wire while leaving a small piece extending from the knot. Paint the end of the wire extruding from the knot with clear nail varnish to prevent it unravelling.

3 Using the flat-nose pliers, place this end of the wire in a flat ribbon crimp. Close the crimp securely and give it a gentle tug to ensure that the wire is firmly caught in the crimp.

4 Thread on the beads separated by the silver jumprings. When you have used three beads, tie a loose knot in the centre of the wire before continuing with the remainder of the beads.

5 Once all the beads and jumprings have been threaded onto the wire, tie a knot in the end close to the last bead. Trim the wire with scissors, leaving just enough to crimp in the remaining flat crimp. Add a small length of chain to the end of the crimp to act as a bracelet extender.

6 Attach the clasp to the other end of the bracelet. Open the jumpring on the clasp using both the flat-nose and chain-nose pliers. Finally, thread this jumpring through the hole on the end of the crimp and close the ring securely.

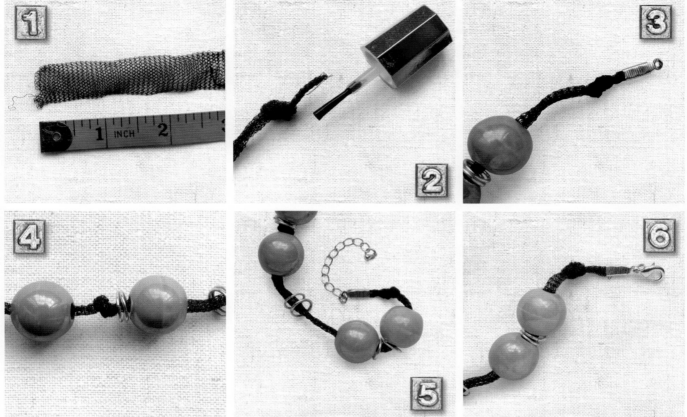

KNITTED WIRE IS FUN TO WORK WITH. IT CAN
BE FILLED WITH BEADS, TWISTED INTO A
VARIETY OF SHAPES AND COMES IN MANY
DIFFERENT COLOURS.

gemma

Fiery red adds some heat

Everything you'll need...

Creative links can be made by combining semi-precious stones and lengths of chain.

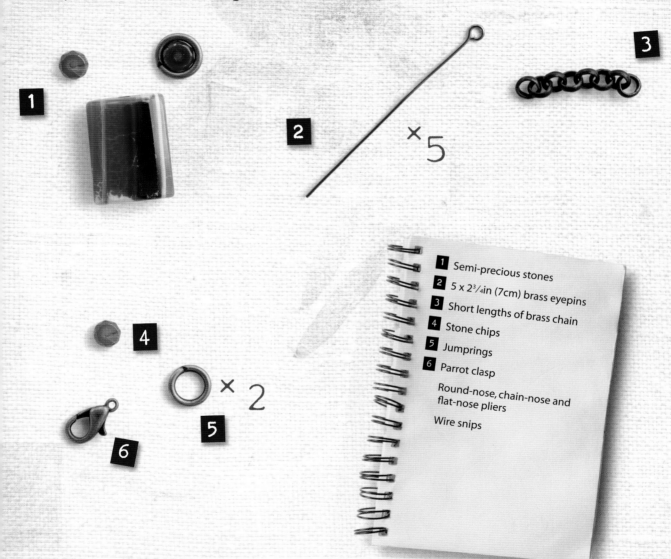

1. Semi-precious stones
2. 5 x 2¾in (7cm) brass eyepins
3. Short lengths of brass chain
4. Stone chips
5. Jumprings
6. Parrot clasp

Round-nose, chain-nose and flat-nose pliers

Wire snips

gemma

Assembling gemma

1 Thread three semi-precious stone chips onto a 2³/₄in (7cm) eyepin followed by a short length of brass chain and a further three stone chips to create a collection of decorative links. When you are happy with the design, make a simple eye at the end of the eyepin using round-nose pliers (see page 18).

2 To make the main bead links, thread an eyepin through a semi-precious stone chip, then a semi-precious stone followed by another chip. Snip off the excess metal on the eyepin, leaving approximately ⁹/₃₂in (7mm). Make an eye at each end of the pin.

3 Repeat this step for all the stones before linking them to the beaded links with jumprings.

4 If you are short of stone chips, or wish to use an alternative, make some shorter links using pearls threaded onto eyepins. Link these to the semi-precious stone links using jumprings.

5 Measure your wrist using a tape measure. When you have finished making the main bracelet, lay it against the tape to check how much chain is required to finish the piece. Use metal snippers to snip the chain, before linking it to the last eye on a beaded eyepin with another jumpring.

6 To finish, add a jumpring to one end of the chain and a parrot clip to the alternative end (see page 13).

THE NUMBER OF LINKS NEEDED
WILL DEPEND ON THE SIZE OF
YOUR WRIST AND THE LENGTH
AND SHAPE OF THE STONES
YOU CHOOSE TO USE.

gemma

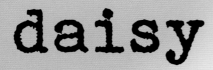

daisy

Cheerful and charming

Everything you'll need...

Use knotted black twine interlaced with hand-painted wooden beads to create a very simple piece that can be made anywhere and in no time at all.

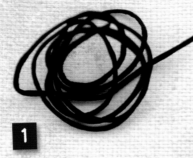

1. Black twine
2. 8 wooden beads
3. Unusually styled button
4. Clear nail varnish

   Scissors

Assembling daisy

1 Cut approximately 39in (100cm) of twine. Fold it in half and hold the fold in the fingers of your dominant hand. Tie a simple knot in the twine, leaving a loop at the end to act as a fastener.

2 Separate the two ends of twine and lay them flat. Pass one end through the centre of a wooden bead. Pass the second strand through the other side of the hole, bringing it out on the opposite side of the bead from where it entered the hole.

3 Thread another bead onto the twine, passing the yarn through the centre of the bead so that it crosses over. Slide this bead towards the first bead to create approximately a 1in (25mm) space between the two beads.

4 Continue to weave the beads onto the two strands of twine. Check the length of the twine against your wrist for the correct size. When you have reached this length, tie the two strands of twine together in a neat knot.

5 Attach a clasp onto the end of the bracelet that doesn't have a loop. Pass the ends of the twine through the holes of an unusually shaped button and tie them into a knot.

6 Cut the ends of the twine so that they are neat and tidy. Finish by dabbing a little nail varnish onto the cut ends to prevent them from fraying.

INSTEAD OF READING A BOOK
TO PASS THE TIME, PULL OUT A
ROLL OF TWINE AND KNOT UP SOME
BRIGHT CHEERFUL BRACELETS.

sky

Composite beads create a classic look

Everything you'll need...

Howlite is a natural creamy white gemstone that, when dyed, looks similar to the semi-precious stone turquoise. Only the price tag will give it away.

1 ×3

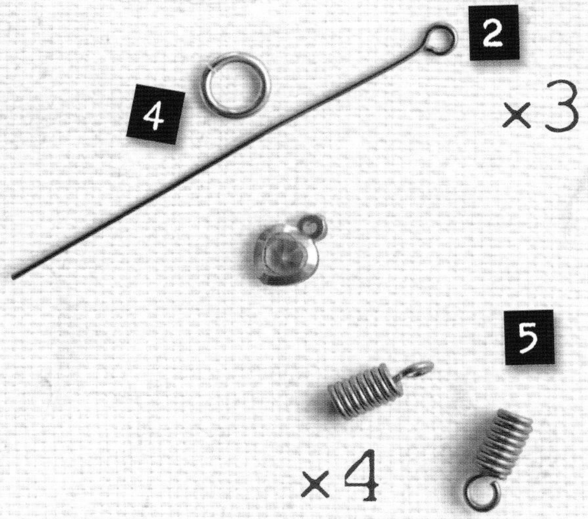

2 ×3

4

5 ×4

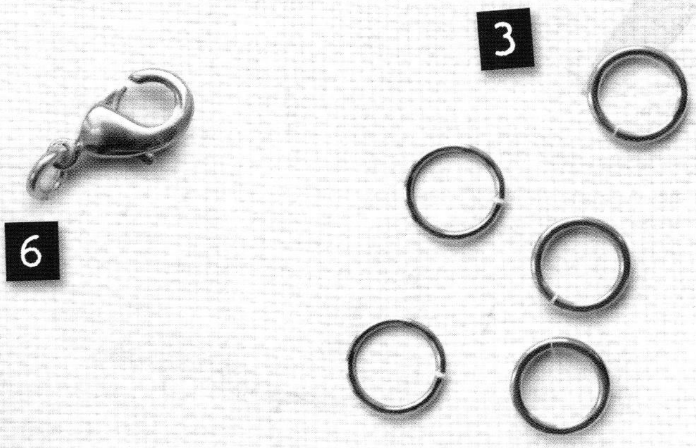

3

6

1 3 howlite gemstones
2 3 x 2¾in (7cm) eyepins
3 5 jumprings
4 Split ring
5 Cord coil crimps
6 Parrot clasp
  Suede cord
  High-strength adhesive
  Flat-nose and chain-nose pliers
  Wire snippers

sky

Assembling sky

1 Lay out the semi-precious stones in a pattern that will become the focal point of the bracelet. Then thread an eyepin through the central stone and make another eye at the free end of the protruding wire.

2 Thread eyepins through each of the remaining gemstones, making eyes at the end of each pin (see page 18). Link the main stone to the smaller gemstones using $5/16$in (8mm) jumprings.

3 Measure the length of your wrist with a tape measure adding on a further $13/16$in (20mm). Lay the linked stones down against the tape to check how much suede cord you will need, then cut the required length.

4 Cut the cord in half and trim the ends into a 45-degree angle with the snippers. Dab a dot of high-strength adhesive onto each end of the cord. Then take the coil cord crimps and twist the 45-degree cut ends into the coils so that the glued ends will help to secure the coiled metal to the suede.

5 Link the two ends of the coil crimps attached to the suede leather with jumprings to either end of the linked beads using the flat-nose and chain-nose pliers (see page 15).

6 To finish, attach a split ring to the end of a parrot clasp using split ring pliers. At the other end of the bracelet, attach a large jumpring to the remaining coiled crimp.

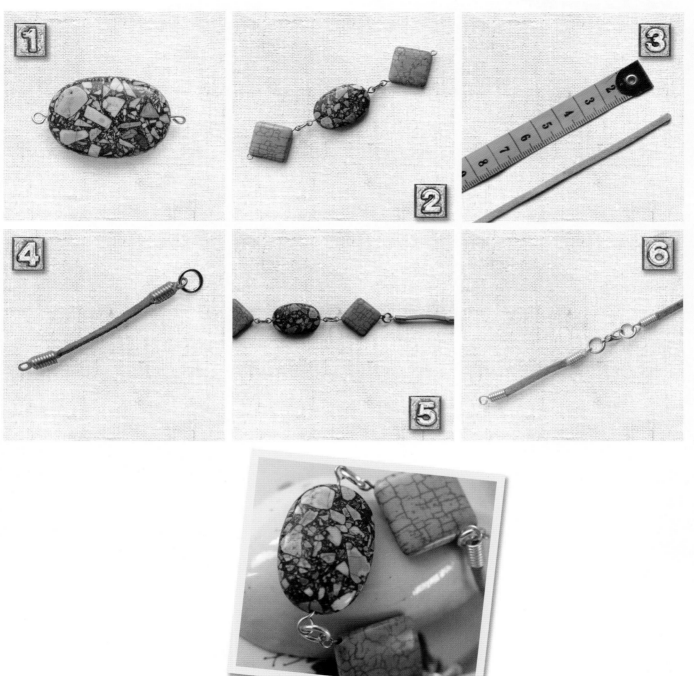

resources

Books

Hot and Cold Connections for Jewellers
by Tim McCreight (A & C Black, 2007)
Jewellery (Two-in-One Manuals)
by Madeline Coles (Apple, 1999)
*Jewellery Making: A Complete Course for
Beginners* by Jinks McGrath (Apple, 2007)
Making Vintage Jewellery by Emma Brennan
(GMC, 2007)
The Art and Craft of Making Jewellery
by Joanna Gollberg (Lark, 2006)
The Art of Resin Jewellery by Sherri Haab
(Watson-Guptill Publications, 2006)
*The Workbench Guide to Jewellery
Techniques* by Anastasia Young (Thames
& Hudson, 2010)
Tips and Shortcuts for Jewellery Making
by Stephen O'Keeffe (A & C Black, 2003)
Wire Jewellery by Kate Pullen (GMC, 2006)

Sources of materials

UK

Beads Direct
21 Gordon Road, Meadow Lane Industrial
Estate, Loughborough, Leicestershire LE11
1JP
Tel: + 44 (0)1656 667 317
www.beadsdirect.co.uk

Creative Beadcraft Ltd
Unit 2 Asheridge Business Centre,
Asheridge Rd, Chersham, Bucks HP5 2PT
Tel: + 44 (0)1494 778 818
www.creativebeadcraft.co.uk

Finding Beads 4 U
www.findingbeads4u.co.uk

Lampwork Cat Beads
(Min Fidler, glassbeadmaker)
www.applegreenmachine.co.uk
www.flickr.com/photos/minfidler

The Bead Shop Scotland
29 Court Street, Haddington, East Lothian
EH41 3AE
Tel: + 44 (0)1620 822 886
www.beadshopscotland.co.uk

Wild about Beads
11B Ewenny Road, Bridgend, Wales
CF31 3HN
Tel: + 44 (0)1656 667317
info@wildaboutbeads.co.uk

Just Beads
Unit 10, Clock House Farm, Lea Road,
Lea Preston PR4 0RA
sales@justbeads.co.uk
Tel: + 44 (0)1772 978 029

Mixed Mediums & Tools, UK
Robin Cameron
Tel: + 44 (0)1929 477 137
mail@cherryheaven.co.uk

Proops
Tel: + 44 (0)1162 403 400
www.proopsbrothers.com

USA

Fire Mountain Gems
www.firemountaingems.com

Rings & Things
P.O. Box 450, Spokane, WA 99210-0450
Tel: + 1 (800) 366-2156
www.rings-things.com

AUSTRALIA

Tools & Beads
Burfitt, 12 Baroola Close, Ocean Reef,
Western Australia 6027
Tel: + 61 (04) 0733 8990
www.burfitt.com.au

Australia Beads
www.divabeadoutlet.com

Beads For Bracelets
Bead Trimming & Craft Co, 139 Merivale St
South, Brisbane QLD 4101
Tel: + 61 (02) 3844 5722
www.beadsforbracelets.com.au

Bead to Craft
156 Bay Tce Wynnum, QLD 4178
Tel: + 61 (07) 3348 5300
www.beadtc.com.au

General

International Craft
www.internationalcraft.com

Beadalon (for threading materials)
www.beadalon.com

Spoilt Rotten Beads
www.spoiltrottenbeads.com

For steampunk jewellery components:
www.earthenwoodstudios.com
www.designersfindings.com
www.timhholtz.com

Useful websites for steampunk inspiration:
www.brassgoogles.co.uk
www.steampunkjewellery.co.uk
www.steampunkguide.com

index

about the author/acknowledgements

Joan is the former editor of UK's leading craft magazine: *Making Jewellery*, a GMC Publication. She is a freelance author, jewellery maker, teacher and designer. Joan has been involved in the craft industry for approximately 30 years. Having worked in an industry alongside a diverse and varied group of artisans she never tires of experiencing first hand new and innovative techniques.

Joan has a passion for creating jewellery and has contributed to many books, craft magazines and DVDs. She is also the author of GMC's *Creative Lampwork* title.

The author and publishers wish to thank Guy Lawrence for his reference photography.

To place an order, or to request a catalogue, contact:

GMC Publications Ltd
Castle Place, 166 High Street, Lewes,
East Sussex, BN7 1XU
United Kingdom

Tel: +44 (0)1273 488005 Fax: +44 (0)1273 402866
Website: www.gmcbooks.com